Robert Cameron Rogers

For the King

And Other Poems

Robert Cameron Rogers

For the King
And Other Poems

ISBN/EAN: 9783744704410

Printed in Europe, USA, Canada, Australia, Japan

Cover: Foto ©Thomas Meinert / pixelio.de

More available books at **www.hansebooks.com**

FOR THE KING

AND OTHER POEMS

BY

ROBERT CAMERON ROGERS

Author of "The Wind in the Clearing,"
"Will o' the Wasp," etc.

G. P. PUTNAM'S SONS
NEW YORK AND LONDON
The Knickerbocker Press
1899

CONTENTS

FOR THE KING.

" *Chief among the captains was*
Adino the Eznite—he lifted up his
Spear against eight hundred, whom
He slew at one time. . . . And after him was
   Eleazar . . . and
After him was Shammah. . . .
. . . And David was in an
Hold, and the garrison of the Philistines
Was in Bethlehem. And David longed
And said: ' Oh that one would give me drink
Of the water of the well of Bethlehem, which is
By the gate!' And the three mighty men brake through
The host of the Philistines and drew water out of the
Well of Bethlehem and took it and brought it to David.
Nevertheless he would not drink thereof, but poured it
Out to the Lord. And he said: ' Be it far from me,
   O Lord,
That I should do this : is not this the blood of the men
That went in jeopardy of their lives ?' "
          2 Samuel xxiii.

FOR THE KING.

I.

Down the steps in the stone that rang
　　To the smite of our feet—
Through the corridors cleft in the rock,
　　Past the guard on his beat,
Under archways rude fashioned and low
　　That echoed and sang
To the jar of our shields—so we ran ;
　　And the sharp brassy clang
Of swords clinking loud on our mail
　　In dim passageways, told
There was something afoot for strong men,
　　To the men in the hold.

II.

Up they sprang from their sleep, catching down each
　　His bow from the wall,
As we ran with the glint of a rising moon's glance

On our shields :

Like a man in a trance stood the guard at the gate
  And let fall

His half-leveled spear in a sudden dismay
  From our path.

We were past him, away in the moonlight,
  And threading the fields

Ere he gathered himself, ere we heard him shout after
  In wrath.

So we ran, all abreast, breathing quick,
  With one purpose in mind—

A draught of cold water to fetch
  From the fountain that springs

In the steep street of Bethlehem,
  Hard by the gate of the town,

For David our master, the Lion of Judah,
  Whose crown

Was assured by the word of the seer
  From the King of all Kings.

III.

It was dark in the valley ; the opposite mountains
  Up-flung

Their black shoulders skyward as farther we ran
  Down the slope,
And the moon was too low yet to cap them—
  In this lay the hope
To cross the bare plain unobserved—
  So we ran in keen haste,
Till, at length, as we halted an instant,
  The jackals gave tongue
Close at hand, and away in the dark
  To their homes on the waste
They scurried in fright, and we knew we were close
  To the plain
Where we fought at the noon with our foes ;
  Where the stiffening slain
Lay unburied.   Then forward, with breath coming
    deeper,
  We ran,
Yet ever and ever again
  We would slacken our speed,
As we stumbled and touched with our hands
  ' What had once been a man,
But whom the Lord in his justice
  Had given to feed

The jackals and foul-feathered vultures
  And kites in their greed.

IV.

At last by the road that ascends
  To the gate of the town,
We halted with common consenting
  And flung ourselves down
To gain breath for a clinch, that we knew
  Was for life or for death.
Then Adino, the Eznite, said hoarsely,
  Still catching his breath :
" Eleazar and Shammah, my comrades,
  The time is but short,
Still a word I must say.   It is like
  We shall not all return.
Hearken now : war has never to me
  Been a shudderless sport.
I have looked in Death's face many times
  And yet never to learn
To make light of my life ;—'t is God's gift—
  Shall I venture to take
His gift as a thing to be lost with a laugh

Or for naught ?

And to-night on this quest, with the peril of death
  Closer brought

Than ever before, here I swear
  There was never a thought

In my heart, of adventure for glory,
  Of foolhardy feat

For women to cry from the housetops,
  The boys, from the street.

I hold such the act of a fool,
  Nay I hold it as sin ;

But to-night ye all saw the sad face
  As I saw it, and knew

How the tide of the past and the wearying present
  Swept through

The heart of the King, till at last, one by one,
  Down his cheek

Slipped the tears—yea the tears, for I saw
  As I stood peering in.

v.

" Then—ye saw it as well—his great hand
  To his forehead he pressed,

Sighing deep as one sighs who cries out
  To himself, in his heart,
' Like a wolf I am driven to cover,
  I seek a retreat
In the dens of the hills, yea I wander
  Outcast, and apart
From a people I served with my best,
  Who of old used to greet
My coming with sackbut and song,
  And the cymbals' loud beat
To the pulse of the voices that praised,
  To the dancers' quick feet ;
And now like a beast of the hills
  I find shelter and rest.
Is it worth all the struggle—to live ?
  And is living so sweet
As the hush of the grave and its peace ?
  Nay, the Lord knoweth best.
He will lead me beside the cool streams,
  He will aid, he will guide.'
Then as though sudden thought of cold water
  Came to him he cried
Quite aloud—though he saw us not :   ,

' Oh had I now but a drop
Of the water that shines in the fountain
By Bethlehem's gate ! '

VI.

" That was all—but enough ; after that
Did I wait, did ye wait ?
Were the heathen as sands by the sea
Should they serve as a stop ?
I hold my life dear, yes I prize it, and
I who have faced
An hundred and flinched not, count life
Far too precious to waste,
But the life that I hold from the Lord
I will give to the King,
God's soldier anointed. A murmur,
A whisper, a word
From him is enough. Ere I cease now
I charge you this thing—
If I fall, as I may, let me lie
Where I perish, but bring
This word back to David : ' His love was so true

That he spent,

Thanking God for the chance, his heart's blood for a
draught

From the spring

That shines by the town-gate of Bethlehem,

Drink for the King.'

Stark and cold though I lie I shall hear,

I shall be full content."

VII.

The Eznite was silent, then suddenly

Shammah spoke out :

"Shall we leave thee, Adino, and bring the draught
home

To our lord ?

Leave thee to the godless, the tribesmen of Gath,

And the rout

Of Anak's foul children ?—Not so—

By the soul in my sword !

Shall it be, Eleazar ?"   I said :

"God forbid it should be.

Die together or bring it together—
  The gift is of three."

VIII.

No word said Adino, but gripped
  Our right hands in his own.
Then we rose and sped upwards, when with a low cry,
  Like a stone
The Eznite stood gazing at each of us
  Panting behind.
" We have brought neither flagon nor skin,"
  He said hoarsely, and each
Looked aghast for a moment, our fettered tongues
  Halting in speech.
Then Shammah laughed low—I can hear him
  E'en now as I tell
A story of years long ago—
  " Will not this do as well ? "
And he took from his head the brass helmet.
  Abroad in the wind
Of the hills his hair floated,—it was yellow
  And bright as the sheen—

There was moonlight at last—of the helmet
    That held it confined.

IX.

Just a glance, just a word—on we pressed,—
    There was need for swift pace—
Turned a bend in the road—quickened speed—
    For the gate lay ahead
Scarce twoscore of cubits—and lo—
    In the moonlight, the face
Of a guard half asleep at his post.
    With a shout he was dead,
By Adino's sword cleft to the chin,
    And our harnesses rang
As over his body and under the arched way
    We sprang—
And hard by the well we three stood—
    As the garrison woke.

X.

"Dip the water," I cried out to Shammah,
    For now a drum beat

And a storm of smooth pebbles flew suddenly by
  In the air—
" Nay," he laughed, " I will fill from the spout
  Where the water is sweet :
It is drink for the King, let it be a fair gift
  That we bear."
Ah, too slow ran the stream—out upon us
  The Anakim came,
Stark spearmen of Ascalon,
  Men of great stature whom Gath
Calls in from the desert—they knew us,
  And cursed us by name :
Ay, cursed us by gods whom we knew not,
  Loud panting with rage
Whilst they hewed, whilst they thrust, but like swift
  Moving sickles of flame
The sword of Adino and mine
  Held them back, keeping broad
A path to the gate. We were wounded
  Again and again,
But for each stroke or thrust we received
  We repaid it in ten.
Yea they fell like the bullocks they slay

To glut Dagon their god,
 Yet they swarmed still the more to their death ;
  They would not be denied,
They had crushed us perchance at the last—
  None too soon Shammah cried,
As with one hand he put back his hair
  That was dripping and dyed
With blood sprung from cuts by the stones
  Flung by men far behind,
" Here is drink for King David," and sprang
  To the gate, and we too,
Hewing, thrusting, and warding, pressed hard,
  Bleeding, panting, half blind
With the salt of the sweat in our eyes,
  Passed the gate with a shout,
Put Shammah nigh swooning between us
  And turned us about
And sped down the hill, while behind us
  The blasphemous crew
Of Anak came racing.   Anon,
  If too near us they drew,
We would turn back, Adino and I,
  Till we slew half a score—

Fresh meat for the jackals of Judah—
    Then downwards once more.

XI.

How we came to the plain with our lives
    Is beyond me to tell,
How we climbed the steep slope to our refuge
    I knew not, nor know,—
But the Anakim ceased at the plain
    To pursue us and fell
To the rear, dreading ambush, and painfully,
    Faltering, slow,
We climbed the ascent to the stronghold.
    About us they ran—
The soldiers of David, wild-eyed,
    Full of questions, each man
Loud mouthed with surprise crying this thing
    Or clamoring that.
They had seen some one pass the gates early
    That night and had heard
The roar in the City of Bethlehem,
    Yet had not stirred

To seek out the cause : to the captains
　　They said, it had seemed
The Philistines were fighting each other,
　　And rat throttling rat
In their den on the opposite hills.

XII.

So the multitude streamed
Up the narrow dim passages, flinty and steep,
　　Of the hold,
And we still went the first, till, behind us,
　　A sudden hush told
That the King was at hand.　In the gloom
　　Just before us, he stood,
And flame of the torches behind us
　　Threw light on his face.
He spake not in words, but his eyes—
　　As, advancing a pace,
He looked at our harnesses, riven and hacked,
　　And the blood
Mixed with dust but half dried on our faces—
　　Gave order to speak.

XIII.

Then each with a hand at his armpits,
    Adino and I
Led Shammah before him,—his knees bending,
    Trembling, and weak
With the spill of good blood—well-nigh spent—
    But a glance in his eye
Like the flash of the soul in his sword—
    And the helmet gripped tight,
His hair, on his neck, like a ripple of brass
    In the light.
Then he held the helm out and he said,
    Clear and high : "Oh my King,
There was rumor that thou wast athirst.
    Here is drink from the spring
By the gate-side in Bethlehem ;
    Yea, and the helmet ran o'er
As I filled it to-night at the spout
    While above me the might
Of these, my two comrades, held Anak's wild
    Spearmen at bay—
As we fought our way back to the hold
    Half was spilled in the way—

Yet 't is cool,—yea, and fresh,—small the gift,
  Would to God it were more ! "

XIV.

Then he lifted the casque and the King
  With both hands seizing fast
Raised it up, said no word, as he stood at full height
  Calm and straight,
But over his visage there came, from his eyes
  There outshone
A look that I saw once of old
  Ere misfortune befell,
When he came to the host that great day—
  That, the greatest of all—
A ruddy-faced youth from his flocks,
  I beheld, I who tell,
And stood by Saul's tent and was armed
  With the armor of Saul.
Yea the same fire blazed in those eyes
  That had gazed calm and wide
On the Giant of Gath coming down
  In his blasphemous pride.
For a moment it seemed he would drink,—

Then another look came
  O'er his face that turned pale 'neath its brown,
    And his eyes lost their flame,
And he turned and sank down on his knees,
    Poured the draught on the stone,
And cried all aloud : " Oh my Lord, oh my God,
    In thy name
I give this, the gift of my bravest—
    Far be it from me
To drink of this draught, 't is their blood,
    It is thine, and for thee."

xv.

Then prone on the ground in the dust,
    With a sob he let fall
That head which the Lord had anointed,
    And suddenly all,
Adino and Shammah and I with the rest,
    Stole away
Down the dark rocky passage in silence,
    Awe-struck at the sight.
So we left him prone-stretched on his face and alone—

As he lay
All about him the hush of the hour
    And the darkness of night—
With the dust in his hair and the
    Bitter unsatisfied smart
Of the thirst in his throat, and the glory of God
    In his heart.

CHARON.

I.

LITTLE have I for which to thank the Gods
Save endless life to endless labor wed.
While Time's slow heart beats out the ages, I
Am bound to toil :—but for one boon to me,
For one surpassing gift, I give Zeus thanks.
For I have heard the sweet, resistless voice,
The cry of passion, quivering through the dusk
To lost Eurydice—yes, one boon more—
That having heard, I found the source of tears.

II.

I too have wept,—but by no pity stung
For pallid shapes that moan upon the thwarts
And stretch their hands back toward the coasts of Life.
Yet I have seen whom Death was loath to lay
His bloodless palm upon ; the man cut down
Before his harvest ; the new wedded wife
Dead ere a mother, and the youth whose eyes
Still found life good, and everywhere delight.

They touch not me.   What harvest has been mine
That I should mourn another's unreaped field?
No wife, no child is mine, and oft I think
That I myself have never been a child,
But have been from the first, as now I am,
Death's ferryman, and next in age to Death.

III.

For them, no tears ; but when amid the rout
Of dull-eyed shades that huddle round my barge
A cowering shadow comes, and, when upon
The farther shore the broad bow upward glides,
Fares forth unmothered, to the gloom beyond,
Some child scarce weaned whose tenure of the world
Was reckoned by the months, who here must weave
His slender thread upon Eternity—
Who never saw the gifts that lie outspread
To childhood, youth and manhood,—then, meseems,
The symbol of my dwarfed and thwarted life
Stands in my gloomy vision, and once more
The wild self-pity clogs my throat,—once more
The sweat is in mine eyes,—again the hour
When first I felt hot tears—the hour whereof
I speak—returns to me.

IV.

One unnamed day—
No day is named on Acheron where all
Alike are sunless, and alike are sad—
I drove my boat from out the farther shore
With one stout thrust, and for a moment stood
Counting the loathsome fee Death's boatman claims ;—
Coins reeking yet of fever-shrunken tongues,
Some dull and rusty, silent witnesses
To violence—and, I remember me,
One bright—as though a mother's thought had laid
A shining coin upon her dead babe's lips—
When, on the wings of one of those shrew winds
That wail incessant down the coasts of Dis,
Came by a voice—a song, a rhapsody—
Sweet, wild, beseeching, desolate, divine,
As though all music of the overworld were dead
And this, its soul, swept sobbing to the fields
Where one sad flower thrives unculled and lone.
Then I was ware—before my senses ceased
To do aught else but drink the magic sound—
That Hell's hoarse turmoil suddenly was still,
That Death's dim valleys lay before me mute,

And in his kennel at the outer gate
The triple-throated yell of Cerberus,
Sinking to sullen mouthings, died away.
The air, so live just now with strident sound,
Hung listening—breathless for the time—the lips
Of the black water round my boat were dumb,
And I could hear what I ne'er heard before,
The beating of a heart within my breast.

v.

There is a word I know, yet never knew
Aught of its meaning—sound alone to me—
Of human speech the word most often spoke
In Hades, for it dies not with the dead.
Even beside the pools of Lethe, those
Who love, and loving die, have turned away,
Nor stooped to drink ; holding more precious far,
The memory of love's mingled cup that broke,
Than those deep draughts that bring oblivion.
Love, love, was all the burden of the song
That held me, old and loveless, wonder-mute,
And though unto my soul no message came
Of love's deep meaning, of love's deathless spell,

I knew immortal music filled my soul
And half divined the power that sped the song.

VI.

So I stood listening, leaning on my oar.
I had not seen that far into the stream
The barge had drifted, and I did not mark
That round about and all along the shore
The noiseless shades had come, some pressing in
Knee deep, thigh deep, yes to the armpits some,
Heedless of those dark eddies.   All were young,
Or had been when Death came, and each one seemed
Alone in some wild concourse of despair.
None marked another's presence,—each one wrapt
In single grief that mourned divided love.
And seeing this, for yet my heart was hard,
I shook my oar aloft and bade them back,
When lo ! the spirit of the music changed
And held me silent with a stronger spell.

VII.

To me it seemed as if some wandering wind
Wet with the tears caught up in passing o'er
A deep, unfathomable, eternal grief

Had veered, and in its place had swept the breath
Of perfect gladness and of pure delight.
Love was the keynote of the singing still,
But love in rapture, in the pride of youth,
Filled full with all that Sun and Earth and Sky—
The gracious Gods whom I have never known—
Cast round their poorest children. Love, indeed,
I may not fathom, but the chord of youth
Through the long darkened chambers of my heart
Rang clear, and into being surged and leapt
The visions of a life denied to me.
I who had never seen the world above,
Had never known the bliss that boyhood knows,
The young blood boasting in the heart, the beat
Of pulses stirring with mere joy of life,—
I whose keen owlet eyes with all their ken
Find naught by gazing but the bleak expanse
Of this dim river—sad-hued heaths beyond,
The sullen realm of Silence league on league,—
I, whose dull, callous ears have never known
Life's morning-music—whom the threnody
Of this blind, sourceless river serves as song,—
Like one who springs from sleep knew, heard and saw.

VIII.

The meadows first—then hills and then the sea
Close by my feet in iteration slow
Carried the burden of Time's earliest song.
Then presently, I thought, a plover called
From sandy sea-crofts, and about my feet
In the warm grass the lesser symphony
Of humbler minstrels rose, and inland, where
The hills toiled up to grassy bastions,
I heard a boy's voice and a pipe that made
Cool interludes of sound 'tween song and song—
And all at once I seemed, myself, the boy,
And shouting ran and leaped and lightly climbed
Along oak-shaded clefts to uplands where
The great deliberate pines bent to the speech
Of winds that urged in solemn monotones.
Far down below I saw the rivers leap
From height to lower height, until at length,
All whirling pearl and amber, foam and deeps,
They pushed to seaward through the level lands,
And I lay prone upon a grassy ledge,
The dipping sun warm gold upon my hair.

IX.

Full-voiced the song swept over Acheron—
And I had given for one such hour of youth
My drear and hateful immortality.
All I had never seen I seemed to see,
All I had never heard methought I heard,
All Zeus had reft from out my life, I knew.
To eyes that never shone with boyhood's fire,
And from the niggard fountain of a heart
That only beat the undertones of life,
I felt the sudden leap of blinding tears
And flung me down upon the thwarts and wept.

X.

And as I lay—my hair flung round my face,
The wire-locks dabbling in the gloomy stream
That seemed to mock in pitiless amaze—
I heard the grating keel, the barge swung round
And lurching slowly, grounded on the shore
That nearest lies to Life.

                Beside my knee
The oar dry-bladed on the gunwale lay ;

Unsteered, unguided, unpropelled by me,
The conscious barge had sought the hither shore.
The song ceased suddenly, and looking up
I saw the singer standing at the prow.

DOUBT.

I.

SLOW groping giant whose unsteady limbs
Waver and bend and cannot keep the path,
Thy feet are foul with mire and thy knees
Torn by the nettles of the wayside fen ;
The dust of dogmas dead is in thy mouth,
Yet down the ages thou hast followed him—
Clear-eyed Belief—who journeys with light heart.

II.

The leaves of Hope about his head are green,
Firm falls his foot upon the path he treads,
To every day he suits his pilgrimage,
And rest at dusk is his—complete and deep.

III.

For thee—the bramble : thorns of vain debate
Harrow the hundred furrows of thy brow :
Sleep is not thine—the darkness has no balm

For thy torn spirit.   Deep into the night
Thy feet that gain no guidance from the stars
Press on, until before the silent tent
Where deep and dreamlessly he lies asleep,
You come with tired limbs to sink beside
The ashes of his fire and find them cold.

LYRICS OF THE GREAT DIVIDE

31

A BALLAD OF DEAD CAMP FIRES.

I.

FOOD for the horses—lots of it—upon the bluff,
Sure to be a spring in a pocket of the hill,
There in the deadfall for a fire wood enough,
Here's the place for bedding down—

Whoa! Stand still!

Throw off the saddles, untwist the hackamores,
Loads off the burro and the pack cayuse :
One shall wear a bell to keep the stock in ear-shot,
Twist the hobbles round their legs and

Turn them loose.

Here on the spot where a fire crackled last year,
Scrape the charry faggots off, kindle one anew ;
Men and seasons out of mind each band that passed
    here,
Lured by feed and water, stopped and

Made camp too.

Sage-brush to kindle with,

Quaking-asp to glow,

Pine-roots to last until the dawn-winds blow ;

Oh smoke full of fancies,

And dreams gone to smoke,

At the camp-fires dead long ago !

II.

Here used to camp with squaws and dogs and ponies,

Long before the coming of the pale-face breed,

Blackfeet hunters, Bannocks and Shoshones,

Laying in their meat against a

Winter's need.

Warm in their blankets, weaving savage fancies

Out of the smoke that veered above the blaze,

Fortunate hunts, the foray and its chances,

New squaws and ponies and the

Head Chief's praise.

.   .   .   .

War parties lurk on the trails to the hunting grounds,

Treachery enters where the tepees spread,

New scalps dry in the Absaroka villages,

The lodge-poles are broken and the
> Fire is dead.

' Sage-brush to kindle with,
> Quaking-asp to glow,
Pine-roots to last until the dawn-winds blow ;
Oh smoke full of fancies,
> And dreams gone to smoke,
At the camp-fires dead long ago !

III.

Here later on came the man whose race is sped and
> gone,
Born white, burnt red under wind and sun ;
Life in the one hand, rifle in the other one,
Traps on every creek in which the
> Beaver run.

Feet to the fire, watching where the eddies spin,
Pine smoke eddies, while the damp logs sing,
Conjuring visions of mighty packs of beaver skin,
Good for gold in plenty at the post
> In the spring.

Trail to the traps in the creek at the break of day,
No trail back—and the sunset is red :
Two eagles wheel above the brush at the beaver-dam,
A timber wolf is howling, and the

> Fire is dead.

Sage-brush to kindle with,

> Quaking-asp to glow,

Pine-roots to last until the dawn-winds blow ;
Oh smoke full of fancies,

> And dreams gone to smoke,

At the camp-fires dead long ago !

IV.

Gone bow and quiver, lance and feather bonnet,
Smooth bore and beaver-trap, buckskin jacket, all—
Here is the stage—but where the actors on it ?
Dead to our plaudits, and the

> Vain recall.

Still one shall hear the coyote in the moonlight,
Still hear the bull-elk whistle up the sun,
Still the old orchestra carrying the tune right,—
Oh wasted music, for the

> Play is done.

We too shall act our parts on other stages,
Spinning out fancies while the Fates spin thread.
Heap up the fire then, keep the present cheery,
We must hit the trail too when the
                              Fire is dead.

    Sage-brush to kindle with,
                    Quaking-asp to glow,
    Pine-roots to last until the dawn-winds blow ;
    Oh smoke full of fancies,
                    And dreams gone to smoke,
    At the camp-fires dead long ago !

THE TETONS AT DUSK.

I.

THE sun has dropped behind the range,
   The twilight saddens hill and tree,
A moment now the world is strange,
   A shifting fairy world to me.
The same terrain spreads mile on mile
   From mountain base to mountain base—
But Nature wears her vision-look
   Upon a changing face.

II.

From early years, of sterner ways,
   On shadowy steeds—from Deadman's Keep—
The spectres of heroic days
   Across a haunted twilight sweep.
Soldier and scout, whose dust, perchance,
   Still drifts about the sage-brush plain,
Keen hunter, eager emigrant,
   Start forth to life again.

III.

A moment—and the silent band,
  Down trails that thread the wastes of Dusk,
Ride back once more into the land
  Beyond the old days' yellow husk ;
And like grim warders of the Past
  The Tetons loom, with shoulders white—
Their mighty backs forever set
  Against the gates of night.

THE PROSPECTOR.

His feet have trod a thousand trails
   That thread the gulch, that climb the slope,
That lead to hope that always fails,
   And yet, gray-haired, he follows Hope.

He walks aloof where highways send
   The stream of frontier commerce down,
From mines whose earliest dividend
   Builds one log store, and names a town.

The mail-stage roars at swinging gait,
   The mule-trains pass with shambling trot ;
Behind his own pack-horse, sedate,
   He sees them and he sees them not.

His thoughts speed on before him still,
   His eyes are to the westering sun,
He asks no odds of Time—his will
   And courage wait at twenty-one.

He knows that Fate has put aside
  His right to plan as once he planned,
Yet strives and will not be denied
  To unclinch Fortune's niggard hand.

The mother, at whose feeble feet
  The golden dust he hoped to pour,
Is dust herself—the hearts that beat
  Quicker for him now beat no more.

Time's sickle keen, Time's vision old,
  Time's sands that mark each hour's span
Are naught to him while flecked with gold
  The dusky pay-sand lines his pan.

His buckskin horse, whose footing sure
  Might tread the bighorn's airy track,
Bears all its master's gear, secure
  With diamond-hitch thrown round the pack.

His wide untiring search has pressed
  Through lone Saguaches' ranges high,
His pick has scarred the triple breast
  The Tetons heave against the sky.

At morn he wets his waking lips
  In streams that join and wax and pour
Beneath the far Pacific ships,
  Where farthest-west seems west no more.

At night he cools his parching mouth
  In waters whose enlarging sweep
Draws through the valleys east and south
  To where the Great Gulf's breakers leap.

And still with ken age cannot dim—
  With heart that leaps toward trails untried,
He seeks Success—who waits for him
  Beyond—beyond the next Divide.

A HEALTH AT THE FORD.

I.

BRONCHO DAN halts midway of the stream,
Sucking up the water that goes tugging at his knees ;
High noon and dry noon—to-day it does n't seem
As if the country ever knew the blessing of a breeze.

    A torn felt hat with the brim cockled up,
    A dip from the saddle—there you are—
It 's the brew of old Snake River in a cowboy's drinking
        cup—
    At the ford of Deadman's Bar.

II.

" Now for a toast, a health before we go—
A health to the life that makes living worth a try ;
A long drink, a deep drink, it 's bumpers, Dan, you know;
No heel-taps now, old pony, you must drink the river dry !

    Here 's to her then—every sunrise knows her name,
    I 've given it away to every star ;
Cold water in a hat !   Pretty tough, but what of that ?—
    It 's the best—at Deadman's Bar.

43

III.

" Where Summer camps all the year by the sea,
By the broad Pacific where your widened waters pour,
Old Snake River, take a message down for me,
Tell the waves that sing to her along the Southern Shore ;
> Say that I 'm a-rustling, though the trail that leads
> > to wealth
> Is mighty hard to find and dim and far,
But tell her that I love her, and say I drank her health
> To-day at Deadman's Bar."

THE MAVERICK.

I.

WHERE at Summer dawn the frost is on the scrub—
Where the prentice-pine and quaking-aspen grow,
 Where the August night is bitter,
 Where the sow-bear leads her litter
From the timber-line zigzag across the snow,
I was foaled in the night, and the sound
 That I heard the first of all
 Was the lean coyote's brawl—
As I lay beside my mother on the ground.

II.

She was bred to the service of the pack—
She was vassal to the hobble and the cinch—
 By the brand upon her quarter,
 By the beaver pelts that bought her,
She was bound to face her game and never flinch.
And her pluck, I have seen it put to proof

When the band swung nose to nose
If the black wolf came too close, ˙
Or fought off the mountain lion with the hoof.

III.

But her heart was broken long before I came—
Break the heart to break the horse—a simple plan—
    And the brand, so naught could sear it,
    Burned its token on her spirit,
Burned its legend of the masterhood of man.
From the horror of the coming of the brand,
    From my mother who had weaned me,
    Where the kind buck-willows screened me
I lay hidden—when they rounded up the band.

IV.

With a thunder of the stock-horse shod in steel,
With the lariats that swung and whistled keen,
    Sped by oath and shout and laughter
    Went the band—the stockmen after—
Down the trail, and left me crouching there, unseen ;
And I lay till the fading of the light—
    Till the night-hawk lower drew,

Till I heard the " Who-who-who "
Of the hoot-owl's jeering question to the night.

v.

In the star-shine and the solitude I found
Where the hill-trails of the elk herd twist and grope
     Through the forest's shag and bristle,
     Where the bull-elks stamp and whistle,
By the licks that lay upon the farther slope :
And I knew when I crested the Divide
     I had found the hidden home
     Where the wild-bunch breed and roam,
In their shoeless, brandless liberty and pride.

vi.

In the morning when the mist was hanging low,
Down a ridge and through a gulch I picked a way
     Where the black-tail deer were cropping
     'Mid the deadfalls—never stopping
Till the sage brush spread before me, silver-gray,
Till I saw the herd that all or none may claim—
     Saw the colts and brood-mares straying,
     Heard the watchful stallions neighing,
Heard my spirit's kindred calling—and I came.

VII.

Through the feast-time and the fast-time of the years,
Through the shift of fate and fortune, and the change,
    Void of curse of cinch and tether
    We foot out our lives together,
With the whole broad mountain region as a range.
So we live and so we dying still shall be
    Free of brand upon our haunches
    As the elk who bears his branches,
As the wolf who drags us down at last is free.

VIII.

Life is living when the living is our own,
Death is better in the wild-bunch than a life
    With a cowboy set astraddle
    Of a heavy Spanish saddle,
And a bit and spur that mangle like a knife.
Death is dying whether got of man or beast,
    And to feed the wolf is better
    Than to wait with foot in fetter
Till the end shall bring the buzzard to the feast.

IX.

Ho ! the moon is slipping down the great Divide.
Ho ! the bosom of the East is showing pale :
    And the smoke from camp fires drifted
    On the wind the dawn has shifted
Warns the wild-bunch from the cover to the trail.
Hark the beat of shoeless feet, hark, away !
    For the sun at noon must find us
    Stretching out the leagues behind us
Noses westward, to the other slope of day.

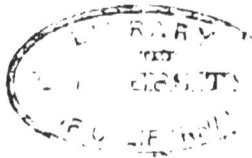

LYRIC ODES

TO SPAIN.

" The Americans are a cowardly race."—Spanish Journal, April, 1898.

I.

WE are not a warlike nation ;
   Here of old our fathers settled,
Seeking scope for their opinions
   In the log-house and the hut ;
Seeking elbow-room and freedom,
   Quiet men but solid mettled,
Almost too religious, maybe,
   Sober-minded people,
               But :

Since they wished to farm the meadows, wished to go to
   church on Sunday,
And the redskin would annoy them with his lust for
   human hair ;
From far Georgia to the South'ard, to the misty shores of
   Fundy,

53

Flintlocks kept the plow a-going, bullets served to
speed the prayer.

II.

We are not a warlike nation ;
　　Though the blood we brought was ruddy
We preferred its cheery runnels
　　In the veins kept tightly shut :
We had thews for farm or fish-net,
　　We had brains to scheme and study,
Brain and brawn for peace and quiet,—
　　That was all we wanted,
　　　　　　　　　　　　But :

Ask the fields by sleepy Concord, ask old wrecked Ticon-
　　deroga,
Of the cost of unjust taxes and old bottles for new wine ;
Something more than glass was broken on the heights of
　　Saratoga,
And the tax was paid at Yorktown by the stiff old buff-
　　blue Line.

III.

We are not a warlike nation,
　　Fashioned rather for keen trading.

Some will say the style is English,
    That from them we get the cut—
East and West our ships went speeding,
    Decks awash from heavy lading,
Bowsprits poked in every harbor,
    Never seeking quarrels,
                            But :

When our rich Levant trade came and Tripoli claimed
    tribute from it,
    Tribute paid by other navies trading down the mid-
        land sea,
We, the least and last of nations, blew her gunboats to
    Mahomet,
    Blew the faithful to their houris, made the Straits
        forever free.

IV.

We are not a warlike nation—
    We had States to form and settle ;
We had stuffs to manufacture
    Till the markets felt a glut ;
We were busy getting headway,

Busy panning out the metal
From the human dust that reached us
From the old-world diggings,
> But :

We could slow up for a moment, just to show our elder
brother
That the bird we put our faith in was not stuffed upon
his perch ;
And we told him through the cannon, in the sea fights'
smoke and smother,
We had searched the Scriptures duly but had found
no " right of search."

v.

We are not a warlike nation—
Peace sometimes keeps men's souls sleeping ;
Some of us still sought a harvest
In the old barbaric rut
Worn by captive feet, till one day
Party spirit upwards leaping
Broke into a flame and blazed on
All the startled nations,
> But :

When the smoke from red fields lifted, when the armies
    were disbanded,—
Better armies, all the world knows, never cartridge bit
    or rammed,—
Proud of their own deeds, and proud too of the men
    who, lighter handed,
Fought them long, and oft-times whipped them, slavery
    was dead and damned.

VI.

We are not a warlike nation ;
    We love living more than dying ;
We have little time for swagger,
    And the military strut.
Let old Europe pay big armies,
    We have better fish for frying,
We have better tools for manhood
    Than the sword and rifle,
                  But :

Since we are a Christian nation, since the blood our
    veins are filled with,
Anglo-Saxon, Celtic, Teuton, will not keep forever
    cool

When we see weak women starving, helpless, ill-starred
  children killed with
  Filthy water, air empoisoned, just to eke out Spanish
    rule ;
Since we find that Cuba's Cuban, and the Spaniard but
  a tenant
  Who defiles the house he lives in, then our duty stands
    out plain ;
We are masters in these waters, at the mainmast flies our
  pennant :
  End this hell on earth or hark ye : Eastward lies the
    path to Spain !

TO GREAT BRITAIN.

November, 1898.

I.

YOUR name is large on every sea
And your keels have underscored
   The title-deed
That the world may heed
How the deed runs, word for word ;
No land so far, no pass so steep,
But the threefold cross wins through,
   Yet we of the West,
   We love you best
For the things you dare *not* do.

II.

Others there be who have strewn their road
With the dust of a deathless dead.
   From the South, from the North,
   Their feet went forth,

And the blood they spent was red ;
Honor was theirs in the harvest days,
And the praise of the Just rang true :
    Till one by one
    They have dared and done
The things that you dare not do.

III.

They talk in the North of a sword laid down,
Of a peace with a world-wide lease :
    But what of the men
    In the exiles' pen
Where death alone brings peace ?
The " Peace on Earth " with a Jew was born—
They have spurned from the land the Jew ;
    And dark at their gate
    The spectres wait
Of the things you dare not do.

IV.

They talk in the South of the rights of man—
They have done with the robe and the crown :
    But Justice pales
    At the clash, in her scales,

Of the sword that weighs them down ;
They look abroad for the leaves of bay
To cover the sprays of rue,
 And they drown with the drums
 The shame that comes
From the things you dare not do.

v.

What seed is this for the lands that lie
To the first stout arm rich prey ?
 What light of hope
 For the years that grope
To the verge of a tardy day ?
"Share," is the cry, " and share alike,"
But your strong sons ask of you,
 " Is it well to share
 With the hands that dare
The things that you dare not do ?

vi.

The hope of the years is the blood we bear,
Are we true to our breed, to our salt,
 If we leave undone
 The work begun,

Though the North and the South cry ' Halt ? '
The furrows we draw are straight and deep,
And ' Truth ' is the seed we strew ;
  With the hand to the plow
  To turn back now
Is a thing we dare not do."

L'ENVOI.

The blood of the West is the blood of the world,
Of a mingled stream come we ;
  But the blood that tells
  Of our hearts' best cells
Is the blood we owe to thee.
We stand to pay when the need shall come,
With the best of the strain we drew,
  Lest the world hark back,
  On an outworn track,
To the things you dare not do.

MISCELLANEOUS POEMS

TO THE RIVER CONHOCTON.

I.

No cradle mid the hills is thine,
No upland pools where earliest shine
The shafts of dawn ; field alders shrine
    Thy mother spring :
From meadow marshes thou art sprung,
From them the music of thy tongue,
From them the charm that makes me young,
    To hear thee sing.

II.

The voiceful trees thy audience
In part are gone—the old offense
Of life lived out—the recompense
    Time asks of each ;
Yet here and yon the sycamore,
The elm and butternut spun o'er
With wild-grape tangles, as before,
    Their branches reach

III.

Above the shallows' noisy sweep,
Above the deeper swirls that keep
A murmurous second, half asleep,
        To praise thy glee ;
And out of sunless days that run
Their untuned hours in the sun,
From shadeless life to-day comes one
        To sing with thee.

IV.

Ah, clear brown water of the pools,
Where mullets drift in lazy schools,
And where the barred-back perch still rules,
        You know me yet ;
For though Time's wanton hand may strip
Man's memory-garden, tree and slip,
Nature, in her companionship,
        Does not forget.

V.

And here of old I used to lie
To watch with an half-dreaming eye

The checkered kingfisher dart by
    With shrill complaint ;
And ofttimes near me, undismayed,
The whiskered muskrat dove and played,
Plying his busy poacher's trade
    Without constraint.

VI.

The dearest memories too that throng
The groves of Youth to thee belong :
There seems a cadence in thy song
    Of soft lament
For him who knew these shores with me,
Who comes no more—nor such as he—
There is a murmur of the sea
    What way he went.

VII.

No measured singing of the waves
To keynotes struck in ocean caves,
No distant hum of gusty staves
    On storm-winds blown,
But that low whisper of the Deep,
The breathing of the tides that creep

'Round beaches where the Greater Sleep
Guards isles unknown.

VIII.

But here, where tripping currents ease
Their speed beneath low-branching trees
To gain in shady silences
    New breath to sing,
Where every alder's dipping stem,
Where every tree that shades thy hem,
And where the hill that shadows them,
    Conspire to bring

IX.

Those memories that grow not old,
Faces that Time must still withhold
From blur, and all the manifold
    Affronts of age,
The changeless boyhood in thy tone
And Youth's spell-song about thee thrown
Make me partaker of thy own
    Rich heritage.

THE OLD BLACK FYCE.

I

His mother was a nameless tyke,
  His sire a mongrel too—
Short pedigree on either side—
  And no one ever knew

How he came by the deep-set eye,
  The trick of nose to ground,
A fyce in shape and color,
  In heart and scent, a hound.

Ten seasons he has followed
  Wherever antlers led,
From Saranac to Little Moose,
  Each swamp, each streamlet's bed.

He knows the runways, one and all,
  He knows the salty licks—
No stag in all the woods can teach
  The old black fyce new tricks.

II.

This morning let the young dogs quest,
  Bruce, Reveillé and Turk,
Three clean-run hounds of family,
  But puppies still,—at work.

Away they bolt, as youngsters will,
  Wide range and noisy tongue ;—
The black fyce does not tug his chain—
  He once himself was young !

He knows that last week's cover holds
  A clue that leads to naught ;
He knows a day-old deer-track means
  But scanty food for thought ;

He knows that puppies must be duped,
  Before they learn to know.
Ha ! Bruce has picked a fresh trail up—
  Now let the black fyce go.

III.

He shakes his rusty doublet,
  His old tail raps my knee,

The chain from off his collar
   Clinks down, and he is free.

Slowly he goes, old age and he
   Are coupled in the hunt,
But Slowpace, running straight, will show
   The soonest at the front.

Away they go—through sugar snow,
   Down slippery swales they yell,
And urging on the flying buck
   The deep-mouthed echoes bell.

Speed, White-tail!   There is call for speed ;
   Swim the cold pond-holes through :
The old black fyce has found thy trail—
   And death and life run too !

STAR-RISE.

I.

AGAINST the afterglow a bat
Draws fleeting zigzag lines ;
The fireflies swing their censers at
A thousand aery shrines.

II.

The woody paths are dim and wet,
The dew lies on the croft,
And, like a glittering vidette,
The first star rides aloft.

A SONG OF THE EAST-WIND.

I.

A SONG of the wind that loves the sea ;—
    The salt East-Wind whose seeking eyes,
Gray as the mid-sea spaces bare,
Peer from the rack of his floating hair
    That streams before him as he flies.

.   .   .   .

A mile beyond the breaking seas
The East-Wind met the Off-shore Breeze.

II.

" Thy breath," he said, " with grass is sweet,
    Thy hair with blown fruit-blossoms white ;
The dew in the tree-tops bathes thy feet—
    Ah, would thy paths were mine to-night !

" For I am weary of mine own,
    No harvests deck the star-sown waste,

73

And kisses from the sea-lips thrown
  Are like to tears,—and bitter taste.

" Old nameless sorrows set the key
  Where ebb-tides draw, and flood-tides reach ;
Where rollers sweep in middle-sea,
  And breakers bend along the beach.

" Then give me title for one day,
  Thy slumberous fields and pleasant woods
To tithe and spoil and kiss, I pray ;
  Ward thou, the while, my realm of moods.

" Ah, let me twine about my head
  The rifled blossoms that you wear,
Let dew, from orchard branches shed,
  Drench both my cheeks, and cool my hair.

" And I shall hark while young larks learn
  The songs that sea-birds may not know,
And I shall watch the sunset burn
  In lands where tall ships never go."

III.

A mile beyond the breaking seas
The East-Wind found the Off-shore Breeze.

" Give back," he said, " my own to me,
   My realm untamed, that mocks at man,
The changeless changings of my sea,
   New-born each day since time began.

" Keep thou thy larks that sing remote,
   Too high to learn thy voice or will—
My sea-birds catch their one wild note
   Close to my lips that whistle shrill.

" Take thou thy blooms of bush and limb,
   Thy perfumes of the woods and downs ;
Sweet is the jar, but at the brim
   Float foul the reeking lees of towns.

" No scoff is mine for Nature's laws,
   Her fields wherein she roams unshod,
But oh the city's stones and stains,
   The deeds that dim the eyes of God !

" Oh sea-lips lift for my emprise,
   Oh kisses salt along my cheek,
Keen as the spray that bites and flies,
   But sweet to him who dares to seek !

" Oh shifting meadows always green,
  Oh leaping hills, that sing with me,
Great heart, world-wide, forever clean,
  I come once more.
                    Give back my sea ! "

IN ABSENCE.

I.

THE sky is blue, is blue, to-day,
The landward hills are green, men say :
I do not know, I cannot see,
For I am blind, away from thee.

II.

Men say the breakers stoop and run
Loud laughing in the noonday sun :
I do not know, I cannot hear,
For I am deaf, save thou art near.

III.

The coverts of the live-oaks sing,
Men say, with tuning notes of Spring :
For me Spring is not yet—thou art
The absent April of my heart.

"TO EACH MAN COMES HIS SEASON."

I.

To each man comes his season : for so long
The little years ran laughing by I too
Came to hold laughter for the only due
Life claimed of me : that mixing in the throng
I too might drift whither such years belong :—
The meadows where no harvest ever stood—
The broad unfruited orchard solitude—
The languid woodlands where no bird has song.

II.

Then came a year of flame whose eager fire
Consumed all little hopes and lit all great,
Blazing across the hill paths hard to climb,   `
Rough hewn among the cliffs of high desire,
And bade me seek where late-grown harvests wait
Secure along the unreaped slopes of Time.

ON A VERSE OF ROSSETTI.

" A little while a little love
May yet be ours who have not said
The word it makes our eyes afraid
To know that each is thinking of.
Not yet the end : be our lips dumb
In smiles a little season yet :
I 'll tell thee when the end is come
How we may best forget."

D. G. ROSSETTI.

I.

I KNOW thy mandates, Love ; none more than I

Have been thy witness and thy willing slave.

And yet for all its power I testify

Thy hand cannot withdraw the gift it gave.

II.

Thou bad'st me hold a purpose half forgot

Dear, since she held it dear ; thou taught'st me this,

To shun all paths in which her feet are not,

To set against the fallow years, her kiss.

79

III.

Thou bid'st me come or go—I come or go,
  So strong thy magic to compel, and yet
With all thy vast puissance well I know
  Thou canst not learn, or teach, the word " forget."

SONG TO SLEEP.

I.

SINCE none may kiss her eyes, save Sleep and I,
Sleep holds himself my rival, and to-night,
Jealous of that he deems his sovereign right,
He will not look on me as he glides by.
What matter then ! his malice I defy—
I 'll dream awake until the waking light,
Dreams winged with longing sent in Sleep's despite,
To haunt her chamber till the dark hours fly.

II.

Sleep, should thy languid kiss her eyelids seal,
Then she will dream and dream alone of me—
But if to kiss them haply shouldst decline,
Her waking thoughts across the night will steal
To meet with mine.   Ah, Sleep, unknown to thee,
I shall prevail whichever path is thine.

IN THE GARDEN.

I.

" Is still the night ? "   " I do not know."
   " Comes dawn ? "   " I do not care.
I only see the golden glow
   That floats about thy hair."

II.

" Do stars still drop from dreaming skies
   Their love-lights to the sea ? "
" Oh, ask me not, who watch thine eyes,
   The only stars for me."

III.

" What whispers through the garden steal,
   Does night, or dawn-wind speak ? "
" How should I know who only feel
   Thy breath against my cheek ? "

IV.

" Not ours to watch Time's shuttles spin:
   My lips on thine let be :
Time is not—Time is lost within
   Our love's eternity."

LOVE'S CUP.

LIFE's richest cup is Love's to fill—
  Who drinks, if deep the draught shall be,
Knows all the rapture of the hill
  Blent with the heart-break of the sea.

Oh tired wings that trail the ground !
  Oh sudden flight to worlds above !
Oh thorns among the roses bound
  About the brows of those who love !

THE STEERSMAN'S SONG.

THE fore-shrouds bar the moonlit scud,
   The port-rail laps the sea—
Aloft all taut, where the wind clouds skim,
Alow to the cutwater snug and trim,
   And the man at the wheel sings low ; sings he—
      " Oh sea-room and lee-room
      And a gale to run afore,
   From the Golden Gate to Sunda Strait,
      But my heart lies snug ashore."

Her hull rolls high, her nose dips low,
   The rollers flash alee—
Wallow and dip and the uptossed screw
Sends heart-beats quivering through and through—
   And the man at the wheel sings low ; sings he—
      " Oh sea-room and lee-room
      And a gale to run afore—
   Sou'east by South and a bone in her mouth,
      But my heart lies snug ashore."

The steersman's arms are brown and hard,
  And pricked in his fore-arms be
A ship, an anchor, a love-knot true,
A heart of red and an arrow of blue ;
  And the man at the wheel sings low ; sings he—
    " Oh sea-room and lee-room
    And a gale to run afore—
  The ship to her chart, but Jack to his heart,
    And my heart lies snug ashore."

SONG.

I BOUND my lute-strings round my heart
    Grown silent long ;
And still as a forgotten art,
    Slumbered my song.

Thy praise, not mine, should favor come
    My songs to seek ;
Thou found'st a dreamer, idly dumb—
    And bade him speak.

I bound my lute-strings round my heart,
    Poor voiceless things—
But thou and Love played well your part,
    And touched the strings.